* * * * * * * * * *

FAMOUS FALSE ACCUSATIONS

* * * * * * * * * * * *

→→► By Virginia Loh-Hagan ◄←←

45TH PARALLEL PRESS

Published in the United States of America by Cherry Lake Publishing Group
Ann Arbor, Michigan
www.cherrylakepublishing.com

Reading Adviser: Beth Walker Gambro, MS, Ed., Reading Consultant, Yorkville, IL
Book Designer: Melinda Millward

Photo Credits: cover, title page: © Andyworks/iStock.com; page 7: British School, Public domain, via Wikimedia Commons; page 9: Palace of Versailles, Public domain, via Wikimedia Commons; page 11: Aron Gerschel, Public domain, via Wikimedia Commons; page 12: File:F. Hamel Stereoskopie Altona-Hamburg 1898 Dreyfuss auf der Teufelsinsel, Bildseite.tif: noch unidentifizierter Fotograf im Vertrieb von F. Hamel in Altona-Hamburgderivative work: Pittigrilliderivative work: Georgfotoart, Public domain, via Wikimedia Commons; page 15: Harper's Weekly, Public domain, via Wikimedia Commons; page 17: Britton & Patterson, CC0, via Wikimedia Commons; page 18: © MIND AND I/Shutterstock; page 21: Library of Congress, Photo by Lee Russell, LOC Control No: 2017744876; page 23: Smithsonian Libraries and Archives, CC0, via Wikimedia Commons; page 25: United Press, Public domain, via Wikimedia Commons; page 27: © paulzhuk/Shutterstock; page 29: © Checubus/Shutterstock

Graphic Element Credits: Cover, multiple interior pages: © marekuliasz/Shutterstock, © Andrey_Kuzmin/Shutterstock, © Here/Shutterstock

Library of Congress Cataloging-in-Publication Data has been filed and is available at catalog.loc.gov.

Cherry Lake Publishing Group would like to acknowledge the work of the Partnership for 21st Century Learning, a Network of Battelle for Kids. Please visit http://www.battelleforkids.org/networks/p21 for more information.

Printed in the United States of America
Corporate Graphics

About the Author
Dr. Virginia Loh-Hagan is an author and educator. She is currently the Director of the Asian Pacific Islander Desi American (APIDA) Center at San Diego State University and the Co-Executive Director of The Asian American Education Project. She lives in San Diego with her very tall husband and very naughty dogs. To learn more about her, follow her on Instagram @vlohhagan.

Note from publisher: Websites change regularly, and their future contents are outside of our control. Supervise children when conducting any recommended online searches for extended learning opportunities.

TABLE OF CONTENTS

* * * * * * * * * * * *

* * * * * * * * * * * *
INTRODUCTION
* * * * * * * * * * * *

Imagine being falsely accused. Something bad happens. You get blamed. You defend yourself. But no one believes you. How would you feel?

Bad things happen. People want to know why. They may blame others. They point fingers. They accuse. These accusations may be true. They may not be true. It's important to have proof.

Some people do bad things. They don't want to get caught. They don't want to get punished. They lie. They accuse others. They use **scapegoats**. Scapegoats take the blame. They're **innocent**. Innocent means not guilty.

False accusations are unfair. They ruin lives. They affect how people are seen. They cast doubt. Learn about famous false accusations in history.

********** CURRENT CASE:

Guilty Before Proven Innocent

****

The Innocence Project is a legal group. Some people are falsely accused. They are wrongly charged with a crime. They may not have money for lawyers. They don't know how to fight the system. They need help. The Project seeks justice. They believe that up to 10 percent of prisoners are innocent, depending on the crime. Most are people of color. A success case was Glenn Ford (1949–2015). Ford was a Black American. He was accused of murder. He was convicted by an all-White jury. There was no proof linking him to the crime. He spent 30 years on death row. Death row is the part of prison where prisoners live before they are executed. The Project took his case. They freed him. They're working on many more cases. About 2,400 prisoners ask for help each year. The Project reviews 6,000 to 8,000 cases. They take cases that can be won with more proof.

* * * * * * * * * * *
ANNE BOLEYN
(1501–1536)
* * * * * * * * * * *

Anne Boleyn was queen of England. She was King Henry VIII's (1491–1547) second wife. Henry wanted a son. Boleyn had a baby girl. Henry turned against Boleyn. He wanted to get rid of her. He wanted to marry someone else.

Boleyn was accused of **treason**. Treason means betrayal. People said she cheated on the king. They said she tried to kill the king. Some people thought Boleyn was a witch. They wondered how she got the king's love. They said she used magic. They said she had 6 fingers. They said she had moles. They said she had a chin wart. They said she had an odd tooth.

The case was weak. There was no real proof. Boleyn denied everything. But it didn't matter. Boleyn was found guilty. She was beheaded.

Anne Boleyn's daughter was Queen Elizabeth I (1533–1603). Elizabeth I was important. She was one of England's best rulers. She ruled for 44 years.

* * * * * * * * * * * *

MARIE ANTOINETTE

(1755–1793)

* * * * * * * * * * * *

Marie Antoinette was Austrian. She was rich. She was royal. She married King Louis XVI (1754–1793). She was the last queen of France. She spent a lot of money. She was unpopular. There were many rumors about her. The French blamed her for their money troubles.

She was accused of many things. People said she plotted with foreign leaders. She made France unsafe. She was an Austrian spy. She sent military secrets to Austria. She was sinful. The list goes on.

Antoinette was jailed. She was questioned.

She gave short responses. She said, "I do not recall." Or she said, "I never heard talk of anything like that." The only crime she admitted was spending money. She denied everything else.

She was found guilty. She was accused of treason. She was beheaded.

Marie Antoinette was called the "Austrian she-wolf." She was also called "Madame Deficit."

* * * * * * * * * * *
ALFRED
DREYFUS
(1859–1935)
* * * * * * * * * * *

Alfred Dreyfus was in the French Army. He was a captain. A letter was found. The letter had military secrets. Dreyfus was accused of spying for Germany. But this wasn't true. Dreyfus was Jewish. People were **biased** against Jewish people. Biased means making unfair judgments. Dreyfus was a scapegoat.

In 1894, there was a trial. Dreyfus was sent to jail. There was little proof. In 1896, new proof emerged. The real spy was Ferdinand Esterhazy (1847–1923). The army wanted to hide this information. But the public wanted justice. Esterhazy was put on trial. He was found not guilty.

Alfred Dreyfus was a captain in the French Army.

Alfred Dreyfus in captivity on Devil's
Island, French Guayana, in 1898

Newspapers wrote of the injustice. In 1898, there was
more proof. Hubert Henry (1846–1898) admitted to
faking proof. He said he set up Dreyfus. Esterhazy fled.
There was a new trial. Dreyfus was still found guilty. It
was unfair. Many people protested. Dreyfus got another
trial in 1906. His conviction was overturned.

★★★★★★★★★★
COLD CASE:
The Unsolved Mystery of the Perth Mint Swindle
★★★★★★★★★

Perth is in Australia. In 1982, there was a robbery. It was called the Perth Mint Swindle. A mint is where money is made. A swindle is a scam. During the robbery, 49 gold bars were stolen. They were worth millions of dollars in today's money. Three brothers were accused. Their names are Ray, Peter, and Brian Mickelberg. They had committed other crimes. They were found guilty of the robbery. They were sentenced to 12 to 20 years in jail. But the brothers didn't do it. They said the police set them up. They said the officers made up their confessions. One officer confessed to making up evidence. The brothers' convictions were overturned and they were released. They were found innocent in 2004. Today, the case is still a mystery. No one knows who did it.

* * * * * * * * * * * *
HAYMARKET RIOT
(1886)
* * * * * * * * * * * *

Haymarket Square is in Chicago, Illinois. There was a protest. It was peaceful. People protested police violence. They supported workers' rights.

Police officers came. They broke up the crowds. A bomb was thrown. People opened fire. There was a riot. Seven officers died. At least one citizen died. Many others were hurt.

Eight men were blamed. Five were German immigrants. They were labor **activists**. Activists fight for causes. There was no proof. Most weren't even at the riot.

But people wanted to blame immigrants. Seven of the men were sentenced to death. One was sent to jail. They were treated unfairly. They were scapegoats. Four of the 7 were executed. One killed himself in jail. The other 2 were jailed for life.

The Haymarket Riot is important. It inspired International Workers' Day. This day is May 1.

SCOTTSBORO BOYS (1931)

* * * * * * * * * * * *

* * * * * * * * * * * *

The Scottsboro Boys were 9 Black teens. They were falsely accused. Two White women lied. They said they were attacked. This happened on a train. It took place in Scottsboro, Alabama.

The accused boys were Haywood Patterson, Olen Montgomery, Clarence Norris, Willie Roberson, Andy Wright, Ozzie Powell, Eugene Williams, Charlie Weems, and Roy Wright. All but 4 were strangers. They did not know each other.

The boys went to court. The jury was all White. It was all male. The boys were found guilty. Most were sentenced to death. They all remained in jail.

The case made the news. It brought racism to light. Some people wanted to free the boys. They hosted protests. They hosted rallies. They wrote letters.

None of the Scottsboro Boys were executed. However, they did suffer in prison for years. All were released or escaped by 1946.

The Supreme Court decided that the Scottsboro Boys were denied the right to lawyers. It also found that the jury was unfair.

The Supreme Court heard the case. It found the boys had been denied the right to **counsel**. Counsel means being represented by a lawyer. The Court also found the jury was unfair.

There were more trials. One of the White women changed her story. But the boys were still punished. They were jailed.

WORST-CASE SCENARIO:

Wicked Witch Hunts

* * * * * * * * * *

Witch hunts are real. Many women were accused of being witches. They were hunted. They were killed. The Middle Ages is a time in European history. It lasted from the 5th to 15th centuries. Thousands of people were killed. There was also a witch hunt in the United States. The Salem Witch Trials took place from 1692 to 1693. Salem is in Massachusetts. Proof of being witches was not based on fact. The accused people had skin blemishes. They spoke their minds. They were different from others. They made others mad. All were falsely accused. More than 200 men, women, and children were accused of witchcraft. More than 150 were found guilty. More than 45 people confessed. Fourteen women and 6 men were executed. These trials were the deadliest witch hunt in U.S. history. In 1693, the Massachusetts governor's wife was accused. The arrests stopped. The trials ended.

Case Six

* * * * * * * * * * *

JAPANESE AMERICAN INCARCERATION (1942–1945)

* * * * * * * * * * *

Japan attacked Pearl Harbor. Pearl Harbor is a navy base. It's in Hawaii. This happened in 1941. The attack was a surprise. The United States declared war. It entered World War II (1939–1945). Japan became the enemy.

The nation felt unsafe. They blamed Japanese Americans. They accused them of being spies. There was no proof. But the government gave into fear. Japanese Americans were taken from their homes. They were forced into **incarceration** camps. Incarceration means being jailed. More than 120,000 Japanese Americans were affected.

No one was found guilty. There were no spies among them. They were falsely accused. Their only crime was looking like the enemy.

The camps were like jails. Armed guards were always around.

EMMETT TILL
(1941-1955)

Emmett Till was a Black teen. He was 14. He lived in Chicago, Illinois. He visited Mississippi. It was summer. He went to a store. He was accused of flirting with a White woman. This was not allowed. The American South had racist laws.

A White mob formed. Emmett was kidnapped. He was abused. He was killed. His body was thrown in the river.

His killers went to trial. They were found not guilty. The jury was all White. It was all male. This was unfair.

People were angry. Emmett's story helped inspire the civil rights movement (1954–1968).

The White woman changed her story. This happened 50 years later. She said, "Nothing [he] did could ever justify what happened to him."

Thousands went to Emmett Till's funeral. This brought attention to racism. His mother had the casket open. She wanted the world to see. She did not want it to ever happen again.

* * * * * * * * * * * *

McCARTHYISM
(1950s)

* * * * * * * * * * * *

Joseph McCarthy (1908–1957) was a U.S. Senator. He was from Wisconsin. The Cold War was from 1947 to 1991. This was a tense time. The United States and Soviet Union were at odds. There was a fear of **communism**. Communist governments own all property. They control what people can do and say. This is different from the U.S. government.

McCarthy made accusations. He called people communists. He called people spies. He said communists were everywhere. He questioned people. He had little proof. But his actions were harmful. People lost jobs. They were rejected by others.

The McCarthy hearings were in 1954. They were a series of investigations. They lasted 36 days. They were on TV. There was a climate of fear.

People spoke out. McCarthy lost support. He died soon after.

The Red Scare was a fear of communists. Joseph McCarthy accused over 200 people of being communists.

* * * * * * * * * * *
JAMES DALLAS EGBERT III
(1962–1980)
* * * * * * * * * * *

James Dallas Egbert III was a child genius. He started college at age 16. He went to Michigan State University. He played *Dungeons & Dragons (DnD)*. *DnD* is a role-playing game. It's a fantasy game.

Egbert disappeared in 1979. He had run away. He killed himself in 1980. He suffered from depression.

Many people blamed *DnD* for his death.

There was panic about *DnD* in the 1980s. Religious groups didn't like it. They thought it was evil. They thought *DnD* was witchcraft. They thought players worshipped the devil. But there is no proof connecting *DnD* to anything evil. It's just a game. It's still played today.

Dungeons & Dragons came out in 1974. Players took on roles. Each player had their own character and game piece.

* * * * * * * * * * *
CHOL SOO LEE
(1952–2014)
* * * * * * * * * * *

Yip Yee Tak was killed. This happened in 1973. Tak was from San Francisco. San Francisco is in California. Tak was a gang leader. He was shot. This happened during the day. This happened on a street in Chinatown. Many Asian people lived there.

Chol Soo Lee was Korean American. He was an immigrant. He was accused of killing Tak. But this wasn't true. He didn't match the killer's profile.

Lee was convicted. He was sentenced to life in prison. He killed another person in prison. He was protecting himself. He was then sentenced to death.

Asian Americans joined together. They wanted to free Lee. Lee won his freedom. This happened in 1983.

Yip Yee Tak was shot on a street in Chinatown in San Francisco, California. Chol Soo Lee was accused of the murder.

FOR YOUR EYES ONLY...

* * * * * * * * * * *

HOW TO BE A FALSE ACCUSER!*

Do you want to be a false accuser? Do you have what it takes? Here are 3 tips:

Tip #1: Be a good liar.

False accusations are lies. Hide the truth. Make up stories. Make up proof. Get the details right. Don't mix things up. Body language may give liars away. Don't break into sweats. Don't twitch your eyes.

Tip #2: Find someone to blame.

Turn attention away from you. Turn it to someone else. Keep distracting people. Hide in plain sight.

Tip #3: Have no sense of right or wrong.

Blaming others is wrong. It should make you feel bad. Ignore the bad feeling.

*WARNING: False accusers can go to jail. They hurt people. Don't falsely accuse anyone.

ICYW: IN CASE YOU'RE WONDERING...

The Science Behind False Accusation

* * * * * * * * * * *

Some people are wrongly accused. They're sent to jail. This is unfair. The most common reason is false accounts. Eyewitnesses are people who see a crime. They recall what happens. Police rely on them. They ask them questions. But eyewitnesses can be wrong. They think they saw something. They accuse the wrong people. Such accounts can't always be trusted. They're based on memories. Memory is not a video recorder. Most people can't recall all details. Memories are affected by many things. Memories can also change with time. Accounts can also be based on bias. Some people may have an idea of what a criminal looks like. They use those ideas to accuse people. They don't focus on the facts. They focus on their own opinions.

GLOSSARY

activists (AK-tih-vists) people who work for political or social change

biased (BY-uhst) unfairly prejudiced against someone or something

communism (KAHM-yuh-nih-zuhm) a government in which goods and services are owned communally; opposite of democracy and capitalism

counsel (KOWN-suhl) a lawyer who represents a person or company in a legal matter

incarceration (in-kar-suh-RAY-shuhn) the state of being confined in prison

innocent (IH-nuh-suhnt) not guilty, free of blame

scapegoats (SKAYP-gohtz) people blamed for things they didn't do

treason (TREE-zuhn) the crime of betraying one's country

LEARN MORE!

Brown, Jordan D. *Fooled Ya!: How Your Brain Gets Tricked by Optical Illusions, Magicians, Hoaxes & More*. Lake Forest, CA: Moondance Press, 2017.

Lawrence, Sandra. *Hideous History: Trials and Trickery*. New York , NY: Little Bee Books, 2016.

Orr, Tamra B. *Crime Scene Investigator*. Ann Arbor, MI: Cherry Lake Publishing, 2016.

Parks, Peggy J. *DNA Evidence and Investigation*. San Diego, CA: Reference Point Press, 2010.

INDEX